THE OLYMPICS

MODERN
OLYMPIC
GAMES

REVISED AND UPDATED

Haydn Middleton

THE OLYMPIC SPIRIT

The modern Olympic Games
began in 1896. Since then the
Game's organizers have tried to
ensure that every competitor
keeps to the true Olympic spirit.
This spirit is based on fair play,
international friendship, a love
of sport purely for its own
sake, and the ideal that it
is more important to take
part than to win.

Heinemann Library
Chicago, Illinois

© 2008 Heinemann Library
A division of Reed Elsevier Inc.
Chicago, Illinois

Customer Service 888-454-2279
Visit our website at www.heinemannraintree.com

Designed by Philippa Jenkins
Originated by Modern Age
Printed and bound in China by Leo Paper Group

12 11 10 09 08
10 9 8 7 6 5 4 3 2 1

New edition ISBN: 978-1-4329-0265-0

The Library of Congress has cataloged the first edition as follows:
Middleton, Haydn
   Modern Olympic games / Haydn Middleton.
     p. cm. – (Olympics)
   Summary: Explores the development of the modern Olympic games from their inception in 1896, discussing location, logistics, rituals, events, and who is allowed to participate.
   ISBN 1-57572-453-7 (library binding)
   1. Olympic Juvenile literature.
   [1. Olympics]
   I. Title.
   II. Series: Middleton, Haydn. Olympics.
GV721.53.M56 1999
796.48–dc21   99-24273
                    CIP

Acknowledgments
The publishers would like to thank the following for permission to reproduce photographs:
Allsport: pp. **6**, **7**, **8**, **9**, **11** (left), **12**, **14**, **17**, **18**, **19**, **20**, **22**, **24**, **25**; Colorsport: pp. **11** (right), **23**, **28**, **29**; Corbis: pp. **15** (ZUMA/Axel), **16** (Nik Wheeler), **26** (ZUMA/K.C. Alfred), **27** (epa/GIGI ARCAINI); Michael Holford: p. **5**; REUTERS p. **4** (Clive Rose/Pool); Redux: p. **13** (The New York Times/Doug Mills).

Cover photograph reproduced with permission of AP Photo/Lionel Cironneau.

The publishers would like to thank John Townsend for his assistance with the publication of this book.

CONTENTS

Any words appearing in the text in bold, **like this**, are explained in the Glossary.

INTRODUCTION

The Olympic Games are by far the most important international athletic competition in the world. Every four years they bring together thousands of the world's best athletes. Millions of people have been able to attend the Games and experience the amazing atmosphere for themselves. Billions of people all over the world now watch the Games on television (up to four billion viewers!). But just 100 years ago, no one could have imagined how the Games would develop. The Olympic Games of the 21st century are nothing like the first modern Olympics that began in 1896.

Since 1924 there have been separate Winter Olympics that take place every four years. They, too, have been steadily growing for more than 80 years.

A record 2,508 athletes (960 women and 1,548 men) from 80 countries competed in the 84 events at the Turin Winter Games in Italy, 2006. There were 18,000 volunteers to help make the Games run smoothly. ▼

Over the years, people have posed many questions about the Olympic Games. How much longer can the Olympic Games keep going? Are they getting too big to organize? Are they getting too expensive to run? Yet the Games have not only survived, but they have grown in popularity and scale. This book tells the story of how the Olympic Games began and how they developed into the competition we know today.

OLYMPIC ORIGINS

Although the modern Games began in 1896, they were not the first Olympics ever. Those date back almost 3,000 years—to ancient Greece. The five-day-long Games featured running, combat sports, the **pentathlon**, horseback riding, and chariot races.

There are records of winners dating back to 776 BCE but the ancient Games came to an end in 393 CE, when the Roman Emperor, Theodosius I, banned all non-Christian worship throughout his empire. Since the Olympics were held in honor of the Greek gods, they had to come to an end as well. But just over 1,500 years later, they began again in their modern form.

This ancient Greek vase painting shows the Greek sport of *pankration*—a man-to-man combat in which almost any form of **aggression** was allowed. ▼

5

BRING BACK THE GAMES!

The Games did not start again of their own accord. By the end of the 19th century, many people in the United States and Europe greatly enjoyed sports. Some might even have dreamed of a brand new global Games, based on the ancient Greek Olympics. But one man above all others made this dream come true. His name was Pierre de Frédy, Baron de Coubertin, a French **aristocrat** who was an active athlete himself!

A RELIGION OF SPORT

De Coubertin (1863–1937) was a widely traveled man. In Great Britain he saw how important sports were in the schools. In the United States he admired the highly developed training and coaching programs at the colleges and universities. Sports became like a religion to him. *STOP*

Baron Pierre de Coubertin, father of the modern Olympic Games.

Through sports, he believed, "our body rises above its animal nature." Sporting contests were "the means of bringing to perfection the strong and hopeful youth … helping toward the perfection of all human society."

"Sports," he concluded, "should allow man to know himself, to control himself, and to conquer himself."

Beginning in 1892, he started trying to convert others to his strong faith in sports. His goal was to set up some games where the "youth of the world" could come together in peaceful, character-building competition: a modern Olympics. It was especially important to him that everyone taking part should be **amateur**. The glory of being an Olympian, not money, would be the athletes' reward.

BIRTH OF AN OLYMPIC FAMILY

It might seem surprising now, but at first de Coubertin found little support for his grand idea. Then in June 1894, at a meeting in Paris, he persuaded **delegates** from 12 countries to back his plan to revive the Olympics. The Games would be held in Athens, the capital of Greece, in 1896. Then at four-year intervals, they would be hosted by other major cities. Soon more countries came into this new Olympic family, and an International Olympic Committee (IOC) was set up to organize and control the Games. De Coubertin himself was president of the IOC for 30 years.

The first modern Olympic Games were held in Athens over 10 days in June 1896. An estimated 245 men—from Greece, Germany, France, Great Britain, and other countries—took part in 43 events. Few of the performances were brilliant. In fact, in events like the discus and long jump, champions from ancient times may well have achieved greater distances! But the Games were very popular with the big crowds that came to watch. The world's appetite had been whetted.

This was the official report of the 1896 Games. Athletes from 14 different nations took part.

The Olympic Charter states that "the Olympic Games are competitions between athletes in individual or team events and not between countries." But ever since 1896, nations have competed against one another to gain the most sports success. ►

THE GAMES ROLL ON: 1900–1936

YEAR	WHERE	WHEN	COMPETITORS		NATIONS	EVENTS
			Men	Women		
1900	Paris, France	May 14–Oct. 28	1206	19	26	88
1904	St. Louis, Missouri	July 1–Nov. 23	681	6	13	89
1908	London, England	Apr. 27–Oct. 31	1,999	36	22	109
1912	Stockholm, Sweden	May 5–July 22	2,490	57	28	102
1916	Berlin, Germany	Cancelled due to WWI				
1920	Antwerp, Belgium	Apr. 20–Sept. 12	2,591	78	29	154
1924	Paris, France	May 4–July 27	2,956	136	44	126
1928	Amsterdam, Netherlands	May 17–Aug. 12	2,724	290	46	109
1932	Los Angeles, California	July 30–Aug. 14	1,281	127	37	117
1936	Berlin, Germany	Aug. 1–Aug. 16	3,738	328	49	129

The official Olympic poster advertising the 1912 Games—the first at which nations from five continents (North and South America, Asia, Australia, and Europe) took part.

OLYMPIC GAMES
ᔓ STOCKHOLM 1912 ᔓ
JUNE 29 th — JULY 22 nd.

The table above shows how the Olympic story continued in the 40 years after 1896. As time went on, the Games were organized over a shorter and shorter period. For the earlier Games, the term "disorganized" was closer to the truth. Some competitors were not even aware that the event they were taking part in was part of the Olympic Games. Sometimes, too, **professional** athletes were allowed to compete.

Eventually organization improved, and there were fewer disputes over which events were official and which were not. The fifth Games at Stockholm set a new standard for efficiency, but then the 1916 Games never took place because of World War I. In ancient Greece, this would not have happened. Back then, a **truce** would have been declared to let the athletes travel to the Games and compete in safety.

8

▶ The men's 4x400 meter relay at the Berlin Olympics of 1936 was the first event to be shown on television. Berliners could watch the Games for free on giant screens in the city's theaters.

GAMES BETWEEN THE WARS

The Olympics resumed in 1920. The Games were held in Belgium, which had suffered horribly during World War I. "All this is quite nice," remarked the Belgian king at the opening ceremony, "but it certainly lacks people." The 1924 Games in Paris had bigger crowds, but trouble kept breaking out because the fans were so aggressive in their support. This was definitely not in the "Olympic spirit."

Women participated in **track and field** events for the first time at the 1928 Games in Amsterdam. Before then they had taken part in tennis, swimming, golf, archery, figure skating, yachting, and fencing. At the next Games, in Los Angeles, fewer women *and* men competed. This was partly because it was too expensive for many Europeans to travel to the United States. At that time, making and selling alcohol was against the law in the United States. But the athletes from France and Italy were allowed to drink wine because they said it was a vital part of their diet.

In 1931 the International Olympic Committee decided to stage the 11th Games in Germany. Two years later, Adolf Hitler and his **Nazi** Party came to power in Germany. Despite much protest, the 1936 Games went ahead in Berlin. As a spectacle they were lavish, since Hitler wanted to prove to the world the so-called supremacy (total superiority) of the German people. Again, this was far from the true Olympic spirit. Hitler's influence over the Olympic story extended beyond 1936, when World War II led to a cancellation of the Games until 1948.

TRULY GLOBAL OLYMPICS: 1948-1996

In the 50 years after World War II, the Olympics grew steadily. More and more competitors took part, more countries got involved, and more events were added. This table shows the rate of growth of the Summer Games.

YEAR	WHERE	WHEN	COMPETITORS		NATIONS	EVENTS
			Men	Women		
1940 and 1944	–	Cancelled due to WWII				
1948	London, England	July 29–Aug. 14	3,714	385	59	136
1952	Helsinki, Finland	July 19–Aug. 3	4,407	518	69	149
1956	Melbourne, Australia	Nov. 22–Dec. 8	2,813	371	72	151
1960	Rome, Italy	Aug. 25–Sept. 11	4,738	610	83	150
1964	Tokyo, Japan	Oct. 10–Oct. 24	4,457	683	93	163
1968	Mexico City, Mexico	Oct. 12–Oct. 27	4,750	781	112	172
1972	Munich, West Germany	Aug. 26–Sept. 10	6,065	1,058	121	195
1976	Montreal, Canada	July 17–Aug. 1	4,781	1,247	92	198
1980	Moscow, USSR	July 19–Aug. 3	4.092	1,125	80	203
1984	Los Angeles, California	July 28–Aug. 12	5,230	1,567	140	221
1988	Seoul, South Korea	Sept. 17–Oct. 2	6,279	2,186	159	237
1992	Barcelona, Spain	July 24–Aug. 9	6,636	2,708	169	257
1996	Atlanta, Georgia	July 19–Aug. 4	6,797	3,513	197	271

◄ For the first time ever, the Olympics went to Asia for the spectacular 1964 Games in Tokyo.

WAR AND PATCHY PEACE

Germany and Japan, which were defeated in World War II, were not invited to London's 1948 Games.

There was also friction between countries during the **Cold War** of the 1950s and 1960s when **communist** countries like the USSR and non-communist countries like the United States were rivals.

They saw the Games as a way to prove their governments were superior.

The last Summer Games of the 20th century were held in Atlanta, Georgia, in 1996. The ex-Olympic champion boxer Muhammad Ali lit the Olympic flame. ▶

PEACE AT LAST

There were many types of disagreements between countries in the second half of the 20th century, resulting in some **boycotting** the Games altogether as a form of protest. The International Olympic Committee (IOC) banned South Africa from taking part for 28 years because of its brutal **apartheid** system.

The chart on page 10 shows that only 80 countries took part in the Moscow Olympics of 1980. That was because 65 countries boycotted the Olympics to protest the USSR's invasion of Afghanistan the year before.

By the 1990s, political problems between countries had calmed down enough that a record 197 nations took part in 1996. But that number would grow even more in the new **millennium**.

THE 21ST CENTURY

The first Olympic Games of the new **millennium** were held in Sydney, Australia, in the summer of 2000. A total of 10,651 athletes (4,069 women and 6,582 men) competed in 300 events, making these the largest Games ever. The Games were also special for the British rower Steven Redgrave, who became the first rower to win gold medals at five consecutive Olympics.

NEW RECORDS

The number of women competitors has kept growing in the 21st century. In 2002 the Olympic Winter Games in Salt Lake City, Utah, included the women's bobsled for the first time. The winner was Vonetta Flowers of the United States, who became the first African-American athlete to earn a winter gold.

In 2004 the Olympic Games returned to Greece, the home of both the ancient Olympics and the first modern Olympics. With more events than ever, the Games now included women's wrestling. Women's **saber** fencing also appeared for the first time. Mariel Zagunis of the United States won the gold medal. It was the first United States victory in fencing.

Despite the war in Iraq, the soccer team from Iraq qualified for the Olympic tournament and made it to the semi-finals. This was another of the highlights of the 2004 Games.

◄ The Olympic Stadium in Sydney, Australia, was the centerpiece of the 27th Games in 2000.

▲ The Beijing National Stadium in China, also known as the bird's nest, is the main track and field stadium for the 2008 Summer Olympics.

FUTURE GAMES

Just where will the Olympic Games be held in 2016? More than 20 cities around the world are already hoping they might have a chance to host the Games. The winner will be announced at the end of 2009. Already some cities have expressed interest in hosting the 2020 Olympics! Some of those already believed to be hoping to make a bid are:

Busan, South Korea

Cape Town, South Africa

Copenhagen, Denmark

Philadelphia, Pennsylvania

Prague, Czech Republic

WHERE NEXT?

In 2008, China will host the Olympic Games for the first time ever. Most events will be held in the new, impressive Beijing Stadium. After that, the 2010 Winter Olympics will return to Canada (Vancouver). The 30th Olympic Games return to London for the third time in 2012, when the organizers hope the Games will be bigger and better than ever before.

WHO GETS THE GAMES?

Besides the organization required, it has also been a very complicated and increasingly expensive business to stage the Olympic Games. Greece, the host country of the first modern Games in 1896, wanted them to be staged there permanently. This suggestion was made again in the 1980s, since the cost of organizing each new Games had become so high for the cities involved.

Both times, the International Olympic Committee (IOC) said no: the Olympic Games are truly international, and should therefore be staged all over the world. An added attraction of this is that a Games held in, say, Tokyo has a very different feel and flavor than the one held in Mexico City.

THE OLYMPIC CHARTER

The Olympic Charter is the official set of rules for the Olympic Movement. It says that some of the IOC's goals are: "to encourage the organization and development of sports and sports competitions; ... to fight against any form of discrimination affecting the Olympic Movement; to lead the fight against doping in sport ... and to see to it that the Olympic Games are held in conditions which demonstrate a responsible concern for environmental issues."

◀ In 1993 these delegates from Sydney, Australia, celebrated their winning bid to stage the 2000 Olympics in their home city.

BEST BIDDER WINS

In July of 2001, Beijing was elected the host city for the Games. It was agreed that "a Beijing Games would leave a unique legacy to China and to sports. The Commission is confident that Beijing could organize an excellent Games."

In July of 2005, London finally won a two-way fight with Paris by 54 votes to 50 to host the 2012 Games. Bids from Moscow, New York, and Madrid had already been eliminated. London celebrated the news, even though some Londoners thought the Games would cost a fortune and cause chaos!

In 2007 a survey showed that hosting the Games could bring a lot of money into the country. The survey was given to people from 35 countries around the world. Of those who said they wanted to visit the United Kingdom, one in three said the Games were their main reason for visiting. People who come for sporting events are likely to spend almost twice as long in a country as other tourists and are likely to be younger.

News of London's victory delighted flag-waving supporters who had gathered in Trafalgar Square. ▼

GLOBAL VILLAGE

This is part of the Olympic Village for the 1996 Games in Atlanta, Georgia. The organizers of these Olympics called them "the largest peacetime social event in human history."

To ensure the London bid was successful, the team promised that every competitor at the 2012 Olympic Games and Paralympic Games would have a bed in a state-of-the-art Olympic Village. That's more than 17,000 beds! After the games, the village where everyone will stay is planned to become a district of Stratford City, a multi-billion dollar development project on the former railway yard near the Olympic Park.

VILLAGE OR MINI CITY?

At the earliest modern Games, athletes and officials stayed in whatever quarters they could find. The U.S. team of 1912 stayed on board the ship that had brought them across the ocean to Stockholm. Competitors in Antwerp in 1920 lived in the city's schools—and slept eight to a classroom!

But at the Los Angeles Games of 1932, the first special Olympic Village was built. It was more like a mini city with its own post office, hospital, fire station, and security guards. The guards had instructions to admit no women. There were only 127 female competitors and they all stayed in a Los Angeles hotel. A village was also built for the Berlin Games of 1936, and at Helsinki in 1952 there were two—because the **USSR**-led **communist** countries demanded separate secure quarters for their competitors, partly for fear that they might **defect** to the West.

The building of more recent Olympic villages has helped make host cities better places for their own citizens to live in. In order to erect a village for the Barcelona Games of 1992, a whole stretch of the waterfront was **reclaimed** and developed. Then, after the Games, local people moved into the specially built low-rise apartments and made them their homes.

VILLAGE LIFE

Judo silver-medalist Nicola Fairbrother lived in the Olympic Village at Barcelona in 1992. "You can taste the apprehension in the air," she wrote later, "sense the hopes and the dreams. All the food in the Village was free. You could eat when, and as much as, you liked. Soon the main food hall became like a magnet for socializing.

"I also have vivid memories of the atmosphere walking about the Village. It was like a bond that existed through every competitor in the Village, regardless of color, size, shape, or sport. You could watch African runners lope by, followed by a group of tiny, Hungarian gymnasts and the Chinese volleyball team. There would be the same look in all of their faces. Everyone in the Village seemed united by the incredible experience. Everyone seemed alive."

By 1992 **professional** players were allowed to take part in many Olympic events. The U.S. basketball Dream Team led by "Magic" Johnson at the Barcelona Games included 11 multi-millionaires. Being such superstars, they bypassed the Olympic village and stayed in $900-a-night hotel suites elsewhere in Barcelona.

THE MARATHON: ANCIENT MEETS MODERN

The longest Olympic race is the marathon. It has been a highlight of the men's events in all the modern Games, and since 1984 there has been a women's marathon too. The idea for the race came from an old Greek legend. In 490 BCE the Greeks won a famous victory over the Persians at the Battle of Marathon. It was said that Pheidipiddes, a **professional** runner, then rushed the distance of about 25 miles (40 kilometers) back to Athens to break the good news. "Be joyful, we win!" he declared on arriving—and then dropped dead of exhaustion. Whether the story was true or not, the organizers of the 1896 Games in Athens decided to hold a long-distance race named after the great battle.

LOCAL HERO

The first Olympic marathon was 25 miles (40 kilometers) long. Although it was run mainly on roads outside Athens, it would finish in the Olympic stadium. To the joy of the large crowd waiting there, the first man home was local farmer Spiridon Louis. He finished in a time of 2 hours 58 minutes 50 seconds. It was Greece's only victory at the Games, and local merchants tried to shower Louis with gifts. All he accepted was a horse and cart to transport water to his village.

◄ Spiridon Louis was the first Olympic marathon winner in 1896. Forty years later the German Olympic Organizing Committee brought him to Berlin for the 1936 Games. There he presented to German leader Adolf Hitler a laurel **wreath** from the sacred grove at Olympia, the site of the ancient Olympics. He died in 1940.

MEMORABLE MARATHON MOMENTS

The marathon has rarely been short of drama. In 1904 at St. Louis, Zulu tribesman Lentauw (one of the first two black Africans to compete in the Olympics) was chased off the course and through a cornfield by dogs. He still finished ninth.

The 1908 London marathon began at Windsor Castle and ended in the Olympic stadium at Shepherd's Bush—a distance of 26 miles (42 kilometers). The runners then had to push themselves through another 385 yards (352 meters) around the track so the finish line would be right in front of Queen Alexandra's **royal box**. In all but two of the Games since then, the official marathon distance has been set at 26 miles 385 yards (about 42 kilometers).

In 1960 Rome staged a night marathon, since the daytime heat was just too great. Both that race and the 1964 marathon were won by Ethiopian Abebe Bikila.

In Barcelona in 1992, Mongolian Pyambuu Tuul recorded a time of 4 hours and 44 seconds, the slowest in 84 years. Tuul had been blinded by an explosion in 1978. In 1990 he ran in the New York marathon with a guide's help. A year later, an operation gave him partial sight, so he entered for the Barcelona Olympics. He said he was there not to win but "to show that a man has many possibilities."

The 2004 Athens marathon followed the same route as the 1896 race, beginning in the town of Marathon and ending in Athens' Panathenaic Stadium. In the men's race, Vanderlei de Lima of Brazil was in the lead with less than 4 miles (7 kilometers) to go when a man pushed him off the course. De Lima still managed to win the bronze medal. He was awarded the Pierre de Coubertin Medal because of his true Olympic spirit.

The winner of the third-ever women's marathon, at Barcelona in 1992, was Russia's Valentina Yegorova. Hundreds of friends and neighbors back in her farming village of Iziderkino bought a 30-year-old TV set. They crowded around it in the street to watch her take the gold.

WHICH SPORTS?

How many different Olympic sports can you name? Most people think of **track and field**, swimming, and gymnastics because these sports attract more media coverage than most. But there are many more. In fact, the 2008 Olympics includes 28 sports. That's 302 events in total—one more than in Athens in 2004. There are 165 men's events, 127 women's events, and 10 mixed events. Nine new events will be held, including BMX cycling, steeplechase for women, 10 kilometers (6.2 miles) swimming for men and women, and team events in table tennis.

OLYMPIC SPORTS FEATURED IN BEIJING, CHINA, 2008
Aquatics (diving, swimming, synchronized swimming, and water polo)
Archery
Badminton
Baseball
Basketball
Boxing
Canoeing
Cycling
Equestrianism
Fencing
Football
Gymnastics
Handball
Hockey
Judo
Modern pentathlon
Rowing
Sailing
Shooting
Softball
Table tennis
Tai kwon do
Tennis
Track and field
Triathlon
Volleyball
Weightlifting
Wrestling

▲ Canoeing is a fiercely contested Olympic sport. Kayak events feature paddles with a blade at each end. The paddles in Canadian canoeing have only one blade.

The International Olympic Committee's Program Commission constantly discusses Olympic sports that already take place, and possible new ones for the future. At various Games since 1896, many sports have tried and failed to find a permanent place in the Olympics. The list below shows some of the sports that now belong in the Olympic past.

DISCONTINUED OLYMPIC SPORTS

(Years in brackets show when they were staged)

Cricket (1900) Britain beat a French team made up mostly of Englishmen.

Croquet (1900) France won all three croquet events.

Golf (1900, 1904) In 1904, Canadian golfer and jokester George Lyon became Olympic champion and accepted a silver trophy after walking down the path to the ceremony on his hands.

Jeu de Paume—"Real Tennis" (1908) American Jay Gould won gold.

Lacrosse (1904, 1908) In 1908, when Frank Dixon of Canada broke his stick, British opponent R. G. W. Martin offered to withdraw from the game until a new one was found. The Canadians went on to win the Olympic final.

Motorboating (1908) Briton Thomas Thornycroft won gold in two different classes. Forty-four years later, at age 70, he was selected for the British yachting team at the 1952 Helsinki Games.

Polo (1900, 1908, 1920, 1924, 1936) In the last competition, Argentina won gold in front of a crowd of 45,000 people.

Racquets (1908) Britain won a clean sweep of all the medals.

Roque—hard-surface croquet (1904) A clean sweep for the United States.

Rugby union (1900, 1908, 1920, 1924) Team member Daniel Carroll won gold for Australia in 1908 and then for the United States in 1920. No one else has ever won gold medals for representing different countries.

Tug-of-war (1900, 1904, 1908, 1912, 1920) The first team to pull the other for 6 feet (1.8 meters) was declared the winner. In 1908 teams of British police officers came in first, second, and third.

Art (1912–1948) Until 1948, medals were awarded for works of art inspired by sports. The medals were divided into five categories: architecture, literature, music, painting, and sculpture.

OLYMPIC TRADITIONS

Processions and parades took place at the ancient Greek Games and now they are dramatic features of the modern Olympics. Each new opening ceremony—watched by very large TV audiences—seems to outdo the previous for spectacular entertainment and effects. The procession of competitors is still led by Greece, followed by all the other national teams in alphabetical order, with the host country's team appearing last. In Melbourne in 1956, a 17-year-old Chinese boy suggested that everyone should walk together as a single **multicultural** nation at the Games' closing ceremony. It was a wonderful sight.

THE OLYMPIC OATH

"In the name of all competitors, I promise that we will take part in these Olympic Games, respecting and abiding by the rules which govern them, committing ourselves to a sport without doping and without drugs, in the true spirit of sportsmanship, for the glory of sport and the honor of our teams."

Since 1920 a representative of the host country has taken this oath at the opening ceremony of each Games. Usually the oath-taker is a veteran of previous Games.

MASCOTS

The first Olympic mascot made its appearance at the 1968 Winter Games in Grenoble. It was a cartoon-like character on skis, called Schuss. Since then each Games has had its own mascot that is usually chosen because of a connection with the host country. Popular mascots have included Misha the Bear at Moscow in 1980, Waldi the Dachshund at Munich in 1972, and Cobi the Dog at Barcelona in 1992. Since 1980 the Winter Games have also had

◄ At Barcelona, Spain, in 1992, a crowd of 100,000 people and a TV audience of two billion watched one of the most breathtaking opening ceremonies ever.

TENDING THE FLAME

The Olympic flame was first lit at Amsterdam in 1928, and it burned throughout the Games. Eight years later, the first torch relay was run. More than 3,000 runners brought the "sacred fire" from Olympia, Greece, where the sun's rays ignited it, to Berlin more than 1,800 miles (2,900 kilometers) away. In 1952 for the Helsinki Games, the torch traveled by air for the first time. Twenty-four years later, the flame's energy sent a laser beam from Greece to Montreal, Canada, to light an identical torch. Then in 1996, there was a moving moment when ex-Olympic champion boxer Muhammad Ali, suffering from **Parkinson's disease**, lit the Olympic flame in Atlanta, Georgia.

Since 1920 this has been the official Olympic flag. It was designed by Baron de Coubertin. Today many believe the colored rings represent the five inhabited continents of the world (though many people recognize six inhabited continents), joined together by sports. These five colors were chosen because, in 1920, at least one of them appeared in the flag of each participating country. ▼

MEDAL CEREMONIES

In ancient Greece, all the Olympic winners were presented with olive **wreaths** at the end of the Games. At each modern Games until 1928, victors' medals were also given out at the closing ceremony. Now medals are presented to the winners of each event as it takes place. Incidentally, Olympic gold medals are 92.5 percent solid silver, with 0.2 ounces (6 grams) of gold on top.

The podium or victory stand—with its 1-2-3 positions—was introduced in 1932. Some people think **national anthems** should not be played at Olympic medal presentations. After all, the Games are meant to be international. At Tokyo in 1964, when Abebe Bikila received a gold medal for Ethiopia, the Japanese band did not know the Ethiopian anthem so it played Japan's anthem instead.

MEN ONLY?

In ancient times, very few women were allowed to watch Olympic events. No women at all were allowed to take part in them. When the modern Games began in 1896, there were still no women competitors. Many people believed that women's bodies could not cope with the demands of top-level sports. Some thought, too, that a woman's true place was in the home, not the stadium.

In the 100 years since the start of the Modern Games in 1896, the number of competitors rose from just 245 men to 6,797, as well as 3,513 women. The gap between the number of male and female athletes is closing all the time. Within the next 20 years, will the number of women even overtake the number of men?

WOMEN ADMITTED AT LAST

The earliest female Olympians were golfers and tennis players. American Margaret Abbott won a golf gold medal at a Paris tournament in 1900 without even realizing that she was taking part in the Olympic Games.

The first Olympic marathon for women was staged in Los Angeles in 1984. It was won by American Joan Benoit (pictured wearing a hat) in a time of 2 hrs 24 mins 52 secs. That was an improvement from the first official, pre-Olympic time clocked by a female marathon runner—3 hrs 40 mins 22 secs by Violet Piercy of Great Britain in 1926.

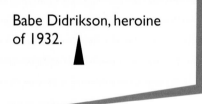

Babe Didrikson, heroine of 1932.

Women made their debut in Olympic athletic events at Amsterdam in 1928. For the first time, women competed in the 100-meter run, the 4x100 meter relay, the 800-meter run, the discus, and the high jump. It was not until 1984 that women were allowed to compete in the most grueling Olympic race of all—the marathon.

A WOMAN CALLED BABE

One woman who did more than most for the cause of female Olympians was Mildred "Babe" Didrikson. At the Los Angeles Games in 1932, this confident 18-year-old American announced:"I came out here to beat everybody in sight, and that is exactly what I'm going to do." She proceeded to win the javelin and broke the world record to win the 80-meter hurdles. In the high jump, she tied for first place and claimed another world record, but received only a silver medal because an official had called her head-first diving style illegal. She would doubtless have won more gold, but women then were allowed to compete in only three events, even though Babe had qualified for five. In later life she excelled in basketball and golf. Someone once asked her if there was anything she did not play. "Yeah," she replied. "Dolls."

FOR THE LOVE OF SPORTS

Amateurs play sports purely for the love of it. **Professionals** get paid to play. Today almost all Olympic competitors are professionals; even top NBA players are allowed to take part. Athletic standards are so high that few athletes could train to the right level and still hold regular jobs. Yet that was what the organizers of the first modern Games wanted them to do. And until very recent times, amateurism remained the Olympic ideal.

A NOBLE TRADITION

"The important thing in the Olympic Games is not winning but taking part. The essential thing in life is not conquering but fighting well." Baron de Coubertin and his fellow organizers of the first modern Games believed very strongly in this point of view. For them, simply taking part was its own reward. There was no question of money being paid, either as a prize for the winners of events, or to competitors for their training expenses. Olympic sports were therefore a glorious hobby for those who could afford to take part.

But the line between amateur and professional in Olympic sports was never completely clear. Spiridon Louis won the first marathon in 1896, and received a simple laurel **wreath** for his achievement. But his fans also promised him a multitude of gifts, including free groceries, free travel, and free haircuts for life. Rewards like these sometimes went to the victors.

Olympic athletes were once meant to be amateurs, but competing in sports these days can be expensive. Starting in the 1970s, the rules began to change, and athletes who trained full-time were allowed to get paid. Now many Olympic stars also receive money to **endorse** products. Snowboarder Shaun White of the United States had many **sponsorship** deals and his own clothing line, even before he won his gold medal.

PARALYMPIC PROGRESS

In the first part of the modern Olympic era, there was no place for athletes who were physically disabled. This seemed unfortunate to Sir Ludwig Guttman, who went on to become the founder of the Paralympics.

In Turin in 2006, disabled athletes competed in five sports: wheelchair curling, Alpine skiing, ice sled hockey, cross-country skiing, and biathlon. Vladimir Kiselev of Russia won the gold medal in the men's sitting 12.5-kilometer (7.8-mile) biathlon competition.

In 1948 Guttman was director of the National Spinal Injuries Center at Stoke Mandeville Hospital in the United Kingdom. His original idea was to hold competitive sports for people with spinal injuries at the Stoke Mandeville Games. Soon people with other disabilities and from other nations got involved, and in 1960 a parallel Olympics began. In that year 400 athletes from 23 countries competed in Rome. This grew to 3,806 athletes from 136 countries competing in 19 sports in the 2004 Paralympics in Athens.

The Paralympic Games have always been held in the same year as the Olympic Games. Since the 1988 Seoul Summer Games and the 1992 Albertville Winter Games, they have also taken place at the same venues as the Olympic Games. Beginning in 2008, the Paralympics will always take place immediately following the Olympic Games, using the same sporting venues and facilities.

The Paralympics are now elite (highest-level) sporting events for athletes from six different disability groups. They emphasize the participants' athletic achievements rather than their disability, and competition is as fierce as in the Olympics themselves.

ICE-COLD OLYMPICS

There was figure skating in the Olympic Games of 1908 and 1920, and ice hockey too was played in 1920. But in 1924 the International Olympic Committee established a completely separate Winter Olympic Games. From then on, including 1992, they were always staged in the same year as the Summer Games, although not always in the same country (see table, right). But beginning with the 1994 Games at Lillehammer, the Winter Olympics were rescheduled to take place in the even-numbered years that fell between the Summer Games.

In the 1924 Games at Chamonix, there were 14 events in five different sports. At Turin in 2006, there were 84 events in 15 different sporting areas.

WINTER OLYMPICS HOSTS
1924 Chamonix, France
1928 St. Moritz, Switzerland
1932 Lake Placid, New York
1936 Garmisch-Partenkirchen, Germany
1948 St. Moritz, Switzerland
1952 Oslo, Norway
1956 Cortina, Italy
1960 Squaw Valley, California
1964 Innsbruck, Austria
1968 Grenoble, France
1972 Sapporo, Japan
1976 Innsbruck, Austria
1980 Lake Placid, New York
1984 Sarajevo, Yugoslavia (now Bosnia)
1988 Calgary, Canada
1992 Albertville, France
1994 Lillehammer, Norway
1998 Nagano, Japan
2002 Salt Lake City, Utah
2006 Turin, Italy
2010 Vancouver, Canada

◄ An exciting moment is captured from the ice hockey match between France and the United States at the Lillehammer Winter Olympics in 1994. In the final, Sweden beat Canada to win gold.

SNOW AND ICE

Far fewer countries send teams to the Winter Games than to the Summer. Countries with warm climates rarely construct ice rinks in which to train future champions. (But at Calgary in 1988, there was, believe it or not, a four-man bobsled team from Jamaica!) The mountainous countries of Europe have dominated the vast majority of the 18 Games. Norway, the **USSR**, Sweden, Switzerland, and Germany have been especially successful in the final medals tables.

Often the Winter Olympians have to compete against the weather as well as one another. Rain, thaw, blizzard, and gale have all created problems. In 1964 at Innsbruck, after a very mild winter, there was simply not enough snow for the Alpine skiing. Austrian troops transported more than 25,000 tons of snow to the River Inn valley from higher snowfields.

One thing is for sure: the Olympics are never dull. What do you think will happen in future Olympic Games?

SPORTS FEATURED AT THE TURIN WINTER OLYMPICS, 2006	
Alpine skiing	Luge
Biathlon	Nordic combined
Bobsled	Short track speed skating
Cross-country skiing	Skeleton
Curling	Ski jumping
Figure skating	Snowboarding
Freestyle skiing	Speed skating
Ice hockey	

◄ Alpine skiing for both men and women is divided into five separate events: downhill, slalom, giant slalom, super-giant slalom, and Alpine combination (downhill and slalom). Here Luxembourg's Marc Girardelli is competing in the downhill at the Lillehammer Winter Olympics.

GLOSSARY

aggression warlike or hostile act

amateur someone who competes for fun, rather than as a job, and who is unpaid

apartheid policy of keeping black people apart from white people

aristocrat member of the upper or privileged classes

boycott refuse to have anything to do with a person, country, or event

Cold War period after World War II of unfriendly relations between the United States and the USSR, which never quite became real warfare

communism political system that has state-owned land, factories, and means of production.

defect leave one country to live in another without official permission

delegate someone sent to a meeting as a representative of another person or group of people

endorse support something

equestrianism riding or performing on horseback

millennium period of 1,000 years. The current millennium started in 2000 and ends in 2999.

multicultural having to do with people who come from different countries and have different ideas

national anthem song written to represent a country and celebrate national pride

Nazi short form of the National Socialist German Workers' Party, a political party led by Adolf Hitler in the 1930s and 1940s

Parkinson's disease illness that affects a person's nerves

pentathlon athletic contest where a competitor takes part in five different events

professional paid competitor

reclaim make land useful or productive

royal box special seats where the British royal family views public events

saber curved sword

sponsorship money given to pay for an event or support a person

track and field sporting events that involve running, jumping, throwing and walking, such as the 100 meter run or the javelin

truce temporary halting of a war or fight

USSR communist country, including Russia and many smaller nations, which broke up in 1991

wreath arrangement of leaves in the shape of a ring

FIND OUT MORE

USING THE INTERNET

Explore the Internet to find out more about the history of great Olympic moments or to see pictures of the most recent Games. You can use a search engine such as http://kids.yahoo.com, or ask a question at www.ask.com. To find out more about great Olympic moments, you could search by typing in key words such as Olympic records, great Olympians, or Paralympics.

These are some useful websites to look at to find more information:

http://www.museum.upenn.edu/new/olympics/olympicintro.shtml
Penn Museum's "Real Story of the Ancient Olympic Games."

http://www.paralympic.org
Home of the IPC (International Paralympic Committee)

http://www.NBColympics.com
Watch the games live as they happen. Also news reports and Olympian interviews.

http://www.USOC.org
The official website of the U.S. Olympic Team.

BOOKS

Gifford, Clive. *Summer Olympics*. Boston: Kingfisher, 2004.

McMullen, Paul. *Amazing Pace: The Story of Olympic Champion Michael Phelps from Sydney to Athens to Beijing*. New York: Rodale, 2006.

Oxlade, Chris. *Olympics (Eyewitness Guides)*. New York: DK Publishing, 2004.

INDEX